Wilderness

Wilderness

Explore the natural beauty of the earth

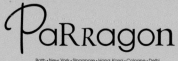

Bath · New York · Singapore · Hong Kong · Cologne · Delhi
Melbourne · Amsterdam · Johannesburg · Auckland · Shenzhen

First published by Parragon in 2010

Parragon
Queen Street House
4 Queen Street
Bath BA1 1HE, UK

Designed, produced and packaged by
Stonecastle Graphics Limited

Designed by Paul Turner and Sue Pressley
Edited by Philip de Ste. Croix

ISBN 978-1-4454-2006-6

Printed in China

Page 1: The Breakaways Reserve in northern South Australia's arid outback is believed to have been formed by the evaporation of an ancient inland sea. The reserve derives its name from the huge rocks which appear to have 'broken off' from the distant mainland.

Page 2: The jagged granite peak of Mount Fitz Roy is the highest summit in Los Glaciares National Park. This ice-covered wilderness in Patagonia, Argentina, contains lakes, mountains, ice caps, glaciers and deserted steppes within an area of some 4460 km^2 (1720sq miles).

Page 3: The vast Eurasian Steppe is a belt of grassland that extends some 8000km (5000 miles) from Hungary in the west through Ukraine and Central Asia to Manchuria in the east. Mountain ranges interrupt the steppe, dividing the great wilderness into distinct segments.

Right: The Okavango Delta in Botswana, the world's largest inland delta, is subject to seasonal flooding. The floods peak between June and August, when the delta swells to three times its permanent size, attracting animals from miles around and creating one of Africa's greatest concentrations of wildlife.

Contents

Introduction

Mountains
The ancient majesty of the world's highest places

Deserts
Vistas of the lone and level sands

Polar Regions
The icy vastness at the ends of the Earth

Plateaux and Plains
High plains and remote uplands

Wetlands and Swamps
Uncovering the watery world of swamps, marshes and bogs

Forests and Jungles
Life in the dense green kingdom of trees

Index

Introduction

When spacecraft return images of the whole Earth at night-time, it is fascinating to trace the network of light sources that sparkle across the globe. The bright spots mark the cities and towns where human beings, who are social creatures by nature, have gathered together to live and work. But, tellingly, huge areas of the Earth appear dark and relatively undisturbed by human activity. In a way it is reassuring to see that parts of the world still preserve their ancient topographies, and that – for all the hustle and bustle of 21st-century life – it is possible to experience parts of the planet as they would have looked and felt thousands of years ago.

This beautiful book makes abundantly clear just how many areas of the globe remain virtually untouched by human activities. These are the true wildernesses – land that is uncultivated and largely uninhabited or, where humans do eke out a living, it is by pursuing a way of life that generally respects and works with the native flora and fauna and employs traditional ways of working that have stood the test of time. For the armchair traveller, this window onto a wild world should prove wonderfully refreshing.

The wildernesses celebrated in the book are grouped into six categories according to their geography and ecology: mountains, deserts, the polar regions, plateaux and plains, wetlands and swamps, and forests and jungles. The photographs offer vistas of startling beauty and majesty. The word 'awesome' has these days become a popular, rather devalued trope, but its use in this context is fully merited – such sights inspire awe. They serve to remind us that the great forces of nature will never be subdued by human activity and that the world's wildernesses will be there to challenge and inspire humankind for millennia to come.

Right: Crystals shimmer on the mirror-like surface of Salar de Uyuni, the world's largest salt flat, set in Bolivia's high plateau region. Countless flamingos may be seen here, and the flocks are at their most numerous in September, striding across the blanched remains of a prehistoric inland sea.

Mountains

This page: At 8848m (29,029ft) high, Mount Everest is the highest mountain on Earth above sea level and is part of the Greater Himalayan range in Asia. It is situated on the border between Nepal and the Tibet region of China.

Opposite: Annapurna comprises a series of peaks in the Himalayas in Nepal. It is a 55km- (34 mile-) long massif of which the highest point, Annapurna I, stands at 8091m (26,545ft).

Right: Mountain peaks glisten white with pristine snow in Peru's Cordillera Blanca. This 'White Range' is part of the larger Andes system and includes 33 major peaks over 5500m (18,040ft) high including Huascarán, at 6768m (22,205ft) the highest mountain in Peru.

Below: Mount Aconcagua in Mendoza province, Argentina, is the highest mountain in the Americas, and the world's highest outside Asia. It rises 6962m (22,841ft) but, despite this awe-inspiring elevation, the climb to the summit by the northern route is relatively straightforward technically.

Left: Cotopaxi is an active volcano in the Andes Mountains, located south of Quito, Ecuador. It is the second highest summit in the country, reaching a height of 5897m (19,347ft). Cotopaxi has an almost symmetrical cone and it bears a glacier – one of the few equatorial glaciers in the world.

Opposite: Cerro Torre, an almost vertical spike of granite, is one of the mountains of the Southern Patagonian Ice Field between Argentina and Chile. At an elevation of 3128m (10,262ft) the jagged peak is the highest in a four-mountain chain: the other peaks are Torre Egger, Punta Herron and Cerro Standhardt.

Far left: The Canadian Rockies offer an ideal habitat for one of the region's most impressive mammals – the grizzly bear. Despite its fierce, predatory appearance, much of a grizzly's diet is made up of berries, roots and other parts of plants.

Left and below left: The Canadian Rockies comprise the Canadian segment of the North American Rocky Mountains range. They differ in composition from, and are geologically younger than, the American Rockies which lie to the south. Unlike their American cousins, they are composed mainly of sedimentary rocks, such as shale and limestone.

Above: Mount Robson is the highest mountain in the Canadian Rockies and is located in Mount Robson Provincial Park in British Columbia. It is part of the Rainbow Range. At 3954m (12,972ft) it is British Columbia's second highest peak. The Robson Glacier which flows off its northeast flank is the source of the fast-flowing Robson River.

Opposite: Mount Rundle, seen here from Johnson Lake, is a 2948m- (9672ft-) high mountain in Banff National Park in the Canadian Rockies. Its dramatic outline was a favourite subject for celebrated Canadian watercolour artist Walter Phillips.

Left: The Mont Blanc Massif mountain range in the western part of the Alps is named after Mont Blanc, at 4810m (15,781ft) the highest summit of the Alps. The range is located in France, Italy and Switzerland. The novelist Thomas Hardy described the Alps as 'shaping like a backbone' the figure of Europe.

Below: The Grossglockner is, at 3798m (12,461ft) above sea level, Austria's highest mountain and the highest mountain in the Alps east of the Brenner Pass. The pyramid-shaped peak actually consists of two pinnacles separated by a saddle-like formation known as the Glocknerscharte.

Left: *The view from the top of Mount Toubkal. This mountain peak in southwestern Morocco is located in the Toubkal National Park. At 4167m (13,671ft), it is the highest peak in the Atlas Mountains and the third highest in Africa.*

Below: *Mount Kilimanjaro in northeastern Tanzania is the highest mountain in Africa and at 5895m (19,341ft) is among the tallest freestanding mountains in the world. Kilimanjaro is a giant stratovolcano that began forming around a million year ago and is composed of three separate volcanic cones. It is no longer active though gases still escape through fumaroles.*

Opposite, right and far right: The Blue Mountains in New South Wales, Australia. The highest point of the range is 1190m (3904ft) above sea level. The mountains got their name because of the distinctive blue atmospheric haze that surrounds them. This is caused by finely dispersed droplets of oil from the many eucalyptus trees that grow on their slopes.

Below: Muztagh Ata, or Muztagata, is the second highest (7546m/24,757ft) of the mountains which form the northern edge of the Tibetan Plateau. This vast and untamed terrain lies on the border between western China and Tajikistan.

Deserts

Below: The Sahara Desert is the world's largest non-arctic desert, and technically the world's third largest desert. At over 9,000,000km² (3,500,000sq miles), it covers most of Northern Africa, making it almost as large as the United States or the continent of Europe. The desert landforms of the Sahara are shaped by wind or by occasional rains, and include sand dunes and dune fields or sand seas, stone plateaux, gravel plains, dry valleys, and salt flats.

Left: Large sand dunes form only a small part of the Saharan landscape as much of it consists of barren, rocky plateaux, which are virtually devoid of sand. Despite its apparent inhospitableness, many animals live here, including camels, gerbils, hares, desert hedgehogs, gazelles and foxes and there are over 300 migratory bird species that populate this area.

Above: Two male springbok antelopes fighting for supremacy in the Kalahari Desert. The Kalahari is a large arid to semi-arid sandy area in southern Africa extending 900,000km² (350,000sq miles), covering much of Botswana and parts of Namibia and South Africa..

Opposite below: The Namib Desert stretches across Namibia and southwest Angola. This ancient desert – it has experienced arid conditions for at least 55 million years – occupies an area of around 80,900km² (31,200sq miles), stretching about 1600km (1000 miles) along the Atlantic Ocean coast of Namibia.

Top: Not all of the Kalahari is true desert – parts of it receive over 250mm (10in) of erratic rainfall annually and are quite well covered with vegetation. The ancient San people have lived in the Kalahari for 20,000 years as hunter-gatherers.

Above: The yellow mongoose is a small mammal averaging about 0.5kg (1lb) in weight and about 50cm (20in) in length. It is a carnivore eating mainly insects, small mammals, lizards, snakes and eggs of various types. It lives in open country from semi-desert Kalahari scrubland to grasslands in Angola, Botswana, South Africa, Namibia and Zimbabwe.

Right: The Gobi is a large desert region in Asia covering parts of northern and northwestern China and southern Mongolia. It measures over 1610km (1000 miles) from southwest to northeast and 800km (500 miles) from north to south.

Opposite: Bayanzag, the 'Flaming Cliffs' of Mongolia's Gobi Desert, are rich in fossils, including those of dinosaur eggs.

Below: The Gobi sustains some animals, including a wild population of Bactrian camels like these. They are one of the few species of mammal that can survive in this harsh desert.

Right: *Rock formations in Death Valley, Atacama Desert, Chile. The Atacama is a virtually rainless desert in South America, covering a 1000-km (600-mile) strip west of the Andes Mountains. Some areas of the Atacama Desert have not had rainfall for 400 years. Normally, it rains every 100 years.*

Below: *These huge petrified tree stumps, scattered over the desert of Patagonia, are all that remains of mighty forests which covered the region 150 million years ago, during the Jurassic Period. They were subsequently preserved by the volcanic ash deposited by massive eruptions in Cretaceous times.*

Above: *Although the Atacama Desert is barren and arid, the tough and hardy guanaco – a relative of the llama – can survive here. Fogs rolling in from the Pacific Ocean are the key to its survival. Dew condenses on cactuses and lichen, which the guanacos eat to obtain the vital water that they need.*

Opposite: *The beautifully symmetrical Licancabur volcano in the Atacama desert lies on the southernmost part of the border between Chile and Bolivia. The summit crater is about 400m (1310ft) wide and contains a crater lake, one of the highest lakes in the world, which is ice-covered for most of the year.*

Opposite: *The Arabian Wahiba Sands are a region of desert in northeastern Oman. The upper areas of the Wahiba contain mega-ridge sand dune systems that are believed to have been created by the action of monsoon winds: Some of these dunes measure up to 100m (330ft) tall.*

Below: *The Arabian Desert is a vast desert wilderness stretching from Yemen to the Persian Gulf and from Oman to Jordan and Iraq. It occupies most of the Arabian Peninsula and its terrain encompasses both huge bodies of sand, like the Rub'al-Khali, and rugged hilly landscapes in the Jebel Tuwaik escarpment.*

Left: *Several species of falcon and eagle live in the Arabian Desert throughout the year. Some, such as the lanner falcon, are captured young and trained by Bedouin falconers to hunt the native bustard and sand grouse.*

Below: *Wadi Rum, also known as The Valley of the Moon, is a valley cut into the sandstone and granite rock in south Jordan. It is the largest wadi (the Arabic term for a valley or dry riverbed) in Jordan. The famous British soldier T.E. Lawrence (Lawrence of Arabia) carried out operations in this region during the Arab Revolt of 1917–18.*

Right: A saguaro cactus grows in Superstition Wilderness, in Arizona's Sonoran Desert. This large, tree-sized cactus has a long lifespan and may take up to 75 years to develop a side branch. Some specimens may live for more than 150 years.

Below: The Mojave Desert occupies much of southeastern California and smaller parts of central California, southern Nevada, southwestern Utah and northwestern Arizona, in the United States. It receives less than 250mm (10in) of rain a year and the temperature in Death Valley during July and August frequently exceeds 49°C (120°F).

Opposite page: Much of Australia is outback, and the largest part of the continent is desert or semi-arid. The red colour of the sand is a characteristic of many Australian desert landscapes. Wildlife has adapted to the tough conditions. Many animals, such as kangaroos and dingoes, rest in the shade of bushes during the heat of the day to stay cool.

Below: A yucca plant grows on a glistening dune at White Sands National Monument, New Mexico, USA. The white sand dunes in this high desert area are composed of gypsum crystals, forming the world's largest gypsum dune field.

Polar Regions

Right: Antarctica is Earth's southernmost continent. It is situated almost entirely south of the Antarctic Circle, and is surrounded by the ice-filled waters of the Southern Ocean.

Below: Paradise Bay in West Antarctica. About 98 per cent of Antarctica is covered by the Antarctic ice sheet, a layer of ice averaging at least 1.6km (1 mile) thick. The continent contains about 90 per cent of the world's ice.

Above: The amazing shapes that irregular and rounded icebergs often acquire is the result of the freshwater ice melting under water, so that when the icebergs sometimes roll upside down, the sculptured forms become visible.

Opposite: Only six of the 17 recognized species of penguin are able to survive in the bleak conditions experienced on the Antarctic continent. They include gentoo penguins (pictured), the third largest penguin after the emperor and the king. They are the fastest swimmers underwater and live on a diet of krill (tiny, shrimp-like crustaceans) and small fish.

Right: The Arctic wolf is one of the few mammals that can withstand the bitter Arctic weather. The white coat is an adaptation to hunting in a snow-covered landscape. They usually travel in small packs, hunting for caribou, muskoxen and seals as well as smaller mammals and birds.

Below: Polar bears live mainly within the Arctic Circle which comprises the Arctic Ocean, its surrounding seas and land masses. It is the world's largest land carnivore and an adult male weighs between 350–680kg (770–1500lb), while an adult female weighs about half that amount.

Right and opposite: The Arctic region consists of a vast, ice-covered ocean, which lies north of the Arctic Circle (the parallel of latitude that runs 66° 33'). In recent years the extent of the sea ice has declined as a result of global warming. Life thrives even in the Arctic and includes marine mammals, birds, land animals, fish, plants and organisms that live in the ice, such as zooplankton and phytoplankton. The Arctic's climate is characterized by cold winters (with average temperatures as low as -40°C/-40°F) and cool summers. Precipitation comes mainly in the form of snow although falls are surprisingly low, with most of the area receiving less than 50cm (20in) annually.

Above and left: *The Arctic tundra is a vast area of stark landscape which occurs in the far northern hemisphere, north of the taiga belt. The word 'tundra' usually refers only to the areas where the subsoil is permafrost, or permanently frozen soil. The soil there is frozen to a depth of 25–90cm (10–35in) and the bare and sometimes rocky land can only support low-growing plants such as moss, heathers and lichen. The tundra experiences high winds, often at speeds between 50–100kph (30–60mph). Animals that inhabit the Arctic tundra include caribou (reindeer), muskox, Arctic hare, Arctic fox, snowy owl, lemmings and polar bears (in the extreme north).*

Right: The willow ptarmigan is a medium-sized gamebird related to grouse. It is a sedentary species, breeding in birch and other forests and on moorlands in the tundra of Siberia, Alaska and northern Canada. Here it is seen in its summer plumage; in winter its feathers are completely white.

Left and below: As the winter snows melt, many plants burst into flower, brightening up the otherwise bare landscape. Flowering plants are supplemented by ground-hugging shrubs, and their blooming spreads a brief but colourful patchwork across the previously barren landscape.

Plateaux and Plains

Right and below: The remote Tibetan Plateau is a vast, elevated area of central Asia that lies between the Himalayan Mountains to the south and the Taklamakan Desert to the north.

Opposite: Sometimes called 'the roof of the world', the Tibetan Plateau is the world's highest and largest plateau comprising arid steppe interspersed with snow-capped mountain ranges, river valleys and large brackish lakes.

Above: *This rock shape, known as 'Arbol de Piedra' (the stone tree), has formed in the Bolivian region of the Altiplano, a high and dry plateau in the Andes Mountains. Strong winds blow across this flat desert landscape, leading to the erosion and sculpting of rocks, as seen here. The Altiplano occupies an area of western Bolivia and southern Peru. It is covered by glacial and alluvial deposits and its rivers and streams drain into Lake Titicaca and Lake Poopó. It is the most extensive area of high plateau on Earth after the Tibetan Plateau.*

Right and opposite page: *The Salar de Uyuni is the world's largest salt flat occupying an area of some 10,582km² (4086sq miles). It is part of the Altiplano of Bolivia in South America and is located in the southwest of the country at an elevation of 3656m (11,995ft) above sea level. The Salar was formed when prehistoric lakes dried out and it is covered by a deep salt crust. It is incredibly flat with the average altitude varying by only 1m (3.3ft) over its entire area. Every November, this wilderness becomes the breeding ground for three species of pink South American flamingos: the Chilean, Andean and rare James's flamingos.*

Right: *The Columbia Plateau stretches across parts of Washington, Oregon and Idaho in the USA. It is located between the Cascade Range and the Rocky Mountains and is cut through by the Columbia River which pours more water into the Pacific than any other river in North or South America.*

Below: *A spectacular display of spring wildflowers grace this magnificent plateau overlooking the Columbia River. The area supports a diverse variety of plants partly because it lies in the transition zone between the moist, heavily-forested west side of the Cascades and the drier grass prairies to the east.*

Left: *The majestic American bison once roamed the grassland of North America's Great Plains in massive herds. However, they were heavily hunted in the 19th century, almost to the point of extinction. The wild population is now carefully conserved and herds of bison are also raised commercially.*

Below: *The Great Plains comprise the broad expanse of prairie, steppe and grassland which lie west of the Mississippi River and east of the Rocky Mountains in the United States and Canada. The prairies support an abundant variety of wildlife including coyotes, fleet-footed pronghorn and prairie dogs.*

Right: A cheetah hunts wildebeest in Masai Mara National Reserve in southwestern Kenya, Africa. Wildebeest abound in this habitat, and their numbers are estimated in the millions. Around July of each year in one of nature's great spectacles they migrate north from the Serengeti plains in search of fresh pasture, returning to the south again in around October.

Below: The savannah and scrub plains of the Masai Mara are home to a wide variety of wildlife including the distinctive Masai giraffe as well as the common giraffe. Lions, leopards, elephants and rhinoceroses are also found here.

Above: The African savannah in Tanzania. Although the savannah is primarily grassland, other landscape features are evident. Besides the grasslands themselves, the most obvious animal habitats are the rivers, rock outcrops and stands of trees which provide shade and safety from predators.

Opposite: The Serengeti Plain is located in northern Tanzania and extends into southwestern Kenya, spanning some 30,000km^2 (11,580sq miles) in area. Around 70 large mammal species are found there, including zebras (pictured), wildebeest, lions, elephants, gazelles, hyenas and buffaloes.

Right: *The Ukok Plateau is a remote and pristine grassland wilderness located in the heart of southwestern Siberia, in the Altai Mountains region of Russia near the borders with China, Kazakhstan and Mongolia.*

Below: *The Eurasian Steppe is a vast grassland plain stretching for roughly 8000km (5000 miles) from the western borders of the steppes of Hungary through Ukraine to the eastern border of the steppes of Mongolia. Steppe regions are typically grassland plains that are virtually devoid of trees.*

Above: *Yaks grazing on the Mongol Steppe in Mongolia. Yaks are widely kept in Asia, primarily for their milk, long coats and meat, and as beasts of burden. They can also draw ploughs. Their dried dung is an important fuel, and is often the only fuel available on the high, treeless Tibetan Plateau.*

Below: *A herd of Bactrian camels on the Ukok Plateau in the Altai Mountains. Bactrian camels are critically endangered in the wild and most of the world's population is now domesticated, like the examples seen here. They are used as pack animals to transport goods across difficult terrain.*

Wetlands and Swamps

These pages: The Okavango Delta in Botswana is the world's largest inland delta. It consists of a labyrinth of lagoons, lakes and hidden channels that cover an area of over 17,000km² (6560sq miles). Located in the arid Kalahari Desert where the Okavango River drains into a basin from which water cannot flow away, it is a haven for the wildlife that depends on the permanent waters of this unique feature, including crocodiles, elephants, hippopotamuses and buffaloes.

Left and below: The Everglades are subtropical wetlands located in the southern portion of the US state of Florida, which experience frequent flooding and drought. The sawgrass marshes form part of a linked system of interdependent ecosystems that include cypress swamps, estuarine mangrove forests and dense stands of tropical hardwood.

Right: Cypress swamps can be found throughout the Everglades. Cypresses often form dense clusters called cypress domes in natural water-filled depressions. The trees in the deep soil at the centre grow taller than those on the outside.

Left: American alligators are native only to the southern United States, where they are commonly found in the wetlands of the Everglades. Adult male alligators are typically 4m (13ft) in length, while adult females average 2.5m (8.5ft). Alligators eat fish, birds, turtles, snakes, mammals and amphibians.

Below: Dawn in the Florida Everglades with cypress trees reflected in rose-coloured swamp waters. Cypress swamps can be found throughout the Everglades, but the largest – the Big Cypress Swamp that is found west of Miami – measures some 3100km² (1200sq miles) in area.

Opposite: An orange sunset sky reflects dramatically in an area of marsh wetland in the Louisiana swamplands, USA.

Left: A white egret hunts for food at the base of a huge cypress tree at Martin Lake, Louisiana. This area near Lafayette is a wildlife preserve and one of Louisiana's major swamplands. It is home to herons, egrets, ibises, cottonmouths, water moccasins, alligators and coypus amongst other wildlife.

Below: A tricolored heron, also known as the Louisiana heron, is a resident breeder in the state's subtropical wetlands.

Above: The largest waterlily in the world (Victoria amazonica) can be seen in the north Pantanal wetlands of South America.

Left and opposite: The Pantanal is the world's largest wetland. This vast tropical wilderness lies mostly within Brazil but extends into portions of Bolivia and Paraguay, covering an area of around 150,000km² (58,000sq miles). Eighty per cent of the Pantanal floodplains are submerged during the rainy seasons.

Below: The semi-aquatic, herbivorous capybara, the world's largest rodent, is common in the wetlands of the Pantanal.

Below: *Tucked away in a corner of the Baltic Sea, to the south of Finland, Estonia is an unspoilt land of extensive forests, wild bogs and ancient grasslands all braided together by an interlaced network of rivers flowing down to a coastline fringed with around 1000 islands. One of the most remarkable examples of untouched wilderness here is the Kakerdaja bog in Albu in the southern part of Kõrvemaa. This area provides a habitat for various protected bird species including the golden eagle, the lesser-spotted eagle and the black stork.*

Left: *The Vasyugan Swamp is one of the largest swamps in the world, occupying 53,000km² (20,500sq miles) of western Siberia. It is home to a number of endangered species. The swamp is a major reservoir of fresh water for the region and several rivers, including the Ob and Irtysh, flow through it.*

Opposite: *The rugged landscape of Connemara in Ireland is largely covered with peat bogs. Such bogs occur where dead plant material, typically mosses and lichens, have accumulated over millions of years in acidic water. These sensitive habitats are home to rare wildlife, including highly specialized native plants.*

Forests and Jungles

Below: The scale and impact of the Amazonian rainforest is truly breathtaking, forming an emerald green carpet of lush forest which follows the Amazon valley to cover an area of about 6 million km^2 (2.3 million sq miles). An incredible wealth of wildlife thrives here in both conventional 'jungle' rainforest and in higher altitude cloud forests.

Opposite, top left: Jaguars once roamed the Americas from the Grand Canyon south to Argentina but today habitat loss and illegal hunting means that this magnificent species is endangered throughout its greatly reduced range.

Opposite, top right: Scarlet macaws are among the Amazon rainforest's most magnificent birds, often flying in pairs above the evergreen canopy in the humid tropics. They may live for up to 75 years but 30 to 50 years is more typical.

Above: Its brilliant plumage and brightly coloured bill make the toucan one of the most easily recognizable inhabitants of the Amazon rainforest. There are about 40 different species of toucan in the world's forests.

Right: The entire Amazon basin flows through nine nations with Brazil claiming by far the largest area – around 60 per cent. The Amazon forest also stretches into Bolivia, Colombia, Ecuador, French Guiana, Guyana, Peru, Suriname and Venezuela. It has been estimated that one in five of all the birds in the world live in the Amazon rainforest, not to mention over 40,000 plant species. There are probably many thousands more species of flora and fauna which are as yet undiscovered.

Right: A juvenile mountain gorilla in the cloud forest of Uganda, Africa. Although mountain gorillas are primarily terrestrial, they will climb into fruiting trees to feed if the branches can support their weight. These highly social primates feed mainly on leaves, shoots and stems and an adult male can eat up to 34kg (75lb) of vegetation a day.

Below: Tropical African forest accounts for 18 per cent of the world's total and covers over 3,600,000km² (1,390,000sq miles) of land in west, central and east Africa. It provides vast wildernesses of arboreal habitats, rich in plants and wildlife.

Opposite page: The tropical Daintree Rainforest in north Queensland, Australia, is home to a huge variety of plants and animals in its 1200km² (463sq mile) range. Some 65 per cent of the bat and butterfly species of Australia and 30 per cent of its frogs, marsupials and reptiles occupy this 135-million-year-old setting – it is the oldest forest in the world. Of the 430 bird species here, 13 are found nowhere else. This is the largest area of rainforest to be found in Australia.

These pages: Temperate deciduous forests consist of trees that lose their leaves every year. They are found in many parts of the world including the United States (above, above right and opposite), Canada, central Mexico, South America, Europe, China, Japan and parts of Russia (right). During the autumn, as the weather gets cooler, the trees begin to shut down the processes whereby they make food, and the green chlorophyll in their leaves breaks down. Then, other pigments show through and the leaves turn beautiful shades of yellow, orange and red before they fall from the branches in winter. These forests provide a haven for wildlife, such as squirrels (far right).

Right: *The cold climate of the taiga discourages many animals from living there permanently. Some of the large mammals found in these northern forests include moose, deer and bears, while smaller animals such as chipmunks also live there.*

Below and centre: *Boreal forests which populate the taiga are characterized by coniferous trees which cover large areas of Canada, Alaska, Sweden, Finland, Norway, the Scottish Highlands and Russia (especially Siberia), as well as northern parts of the United States, Kazakhstan, Mongolia and Japan. The taiga wilderness is the world's largest terrestrial biome.*

Above: *Straddling the Arctic Circle, the wild taiga of northeast Siberia is one of the largest unspoilt boreal forest areas in the world. Much of this cold, remote region is covered by sparse larch forests with an understorey of dwarf shrub-lichen and brushwoods which is home to elk, brown bears and lynxes.*

Left: *The red fox is common in the taiga and it ranges from northern America, Canada and Alaska to northern Europe. It lives in dense woodlands, forests and open country, usually resting in a burrow during the day and hunting at night for small prey animals, such as rabbits, hares and mice.*

Above: The rare proboscis monkey is native to Borneo's mangrove forests, feeding on the plant's shoots and leaves.

Opposite: A mangrove forest in Honduras, central America.

Right: Tropical shores are often lined with mangrove swamps. Salt-tolerant mangrove trees thrive in saline coastal habitats. Their presence helps to protect coastal regions from erosion.

Below: A mangrove forest in Okinawa, Japan. Most mangroves in Japan do not grow taller than 10m (33ft).

Index

Picture credits
a = above, b = below, l = left, r = right, c = centre

© Shutterstock.com
AJancso 50l; alarifoto 52b; alexandern 25bl; Luisa Amare 63r; John A. Anderson 46bl; Anyka 50ar; apdesign 18bl; Ekaterina Baranova 32al; Antoine Beyeler 30cl; Sébastien Burel 2, 11; Lucie Caizlova 44ac; Pablo H Caridad 22b; CJPhoto 25br; CSLD 27l, 27ar, 27br; Louise Cukrov 21; dirkr 44ar; Pichugin Dmitry 3, 8b, 19a, 19bl, 20b, 34a, 42a, 42b, 43a; Dennis Donohue 12al; dusko 30–31r; EcoPrint 18cr, 25a; enote 15b; FloridaStock 47br; Anton Foltin 26ac; Rafal Gaweda 9; Kirk Geisler 39a; hainaultphoto 24; Arto Hakola 47ac; James Harrison 50br; Jiri Haureljuk 4–5, 44b, 45; Lukas Hlavac 8ac; Patrick Hoff 13; Martin Horskey 1; hunta 43b; iofoto 46–47c; Irina B 46al; Rafa Irusta 14r; Eric Isselée 41; Anthon Jackson 17b; Matthew Jacques 32bl; javarman 6–7, 36–37c, 40a; Kjersti Joergensen 63al; kavram 39b; Bill Kennedy 58ar; Kirsanov 60ac, 61bc; kkaplin 28a; Vasiliy Koval 52a; krechet 40cr; Chris Kruger 19cr; Boleslaw Kubica 56r; Michael Leggero 49br; Henrik Lehnerer 54ar; Katrina Leigh 26br; Chee-Onn Leong 16, 17ac, 17ar, 26bl; Ralph Loesche 57al, 57ar; Nuno Miguel Duarte Rodrigues Lopes 18ac; X.D.Luo 34b; Jason Maehl 10cl; Robyn Mackenzie 57ac, 57b; mastiffliu 34–35r; Vladimir Melnik 10bl; Jose Luis Mesa 55al; Ed Metz 48; Mighty Sequoia Studio 12cr; Mike Norton 12ac, 58al; Denis Pepin 30ac; Potapov Igor Petrovich 60bl, 60–61c; Photodynamic 29; Libor Piška 14l; Andrey Plis 15a; Igor Plotnikov 8ar; Patrick Poendl 30bc; Daniel Prudek 58bc; Lorenzo Puricelli 55r; Jeremy Richards 36l; Eduardo Rivero 22cr; aspen rock 58br; Armin Rose 28cr; Elzbieta Sekowska 56cl; Jiri Slama 12bl; George Spade 61ar; Nickolay Stanev 62; Steffen Foerster Photography 37br; Tifonimages 22a, 23; Willem Tims 28bl, 37ar; tororo reaction 63bl; TTphoto 32–33c, 33ar, 33br; UnGePhoto 38a; urosr 37bc; Asier Villafranca 40bl; Medvedev Vladimir 20a; Paul S. Wolf 49l; J.K. York 59; Alexander Yu. Zotov 10ar; zschnepf 38b.

© iStockphoto.com
HiM 54ac; Torsten Karock 51; Morley Read 54b.

© Paul Turner 53.